MAKING

Greeting Cards

WITH

Rubber Stamps

MAKING
Greeting Cards
WITH
Rubber Stamps

MARY JO McGRAW

NORTH LIGHT BOOKS
Cincinnati, Ohio

ABOUT THE AUTHOR

MaryJo McGraw is a nationally known rubber-stamp artist whose work has been featured in leading rubber-stamp enthusiast publications. She has taught rubber-stamp classes for eight years at stamp stores around the country and has conducted demonstrations and classes at all the major national retail stamp shows.

She has been a sample artist for many of the largest stamp manufacturers and has sold her original artwork to several art stamp companies. Her original ideas and techniques and innovative use of materials make her a much sought-after stamping instructor for demonstrations and classes.

Making Greeting Cards With Rubber Stamps. Copyright © 1997 by MaryJo McGraw. Manufactured in China. All rights reserved. No part of this book may be reproduced in any form or by any electronic or mechanical means including information storage and retrieval systems without permission in writing from the publisher, except by a reviewer, who may quote brief passages in a review. Published by North Light Books, an imprint of F&W Publications, Inc., 1507 Dana Avenue, Cincinnati, Ohio 45207. (800) 289-0963. First edition.

Other fine North Light Books are available from your local bookstore or direct from the publisher.

01 00 99   7 6 5

Library of Congress Cataloging-in-Publication Data

McGraw, MaryJo
    Making greeting cards with rubber stamps / by MaryJo McGraw.
        p.   cm.
    Includes index.
    ISBN 0-89134-713-5 (alk. paper)
    1. Rubber stamp printing. 2. Greeting cards. I. Title.
TT867.M35   1997
745.594′ 1—dc20   96-32192
                                                    CIP

Edited by Joyce Dolan
Designed by Angela Lennert Wilcox
Cover Photography by Pamela Monfort Braun,
Bronze Photography

METRIC CONVERSION CHART		
TO CONVERT	TO	MULTIPLY BY
Inches	Centimeters	2.54
Centimeters	Inches	0.4
Feet	Centimeters	30.5
Centimeters	Feet	0.03
Yards	Meters	0.9
Meters	Yards	1.1
Sq. Inches	Sq. Centimeters	6.45
Sq. Centimeters	Sq. Inches	0.16
Sq. Feet	Sq. Meters	0.09
Sq. Meters	Sq. Feet	10.8
Sq. Yards	Sq. Meters	0.8
Sq. Meters	Sq. Yards	1.2
Pounds	Kilograms	0.45
Kilograms	Pounds	2.2
Ounces	Grams	28.4
Grams	Ounces	0.04

I would like to thank my family and all my good friends for the wonderful support they've shown me during the creation of this book, especially Judi Watanabe, Rob Bostick and Elaine Madrid. Without their patience and help I would have never finished this book. Also the folks at North Light Books, Greg Albert and Joyce Dolan, for their invaluable contribution. My last and biggest thank-you goes to my daughter Chelsea for all her help—whether lugging a box of stuff for classes or cleaning stamps, she's always there to help with the little things.

Table of Contents

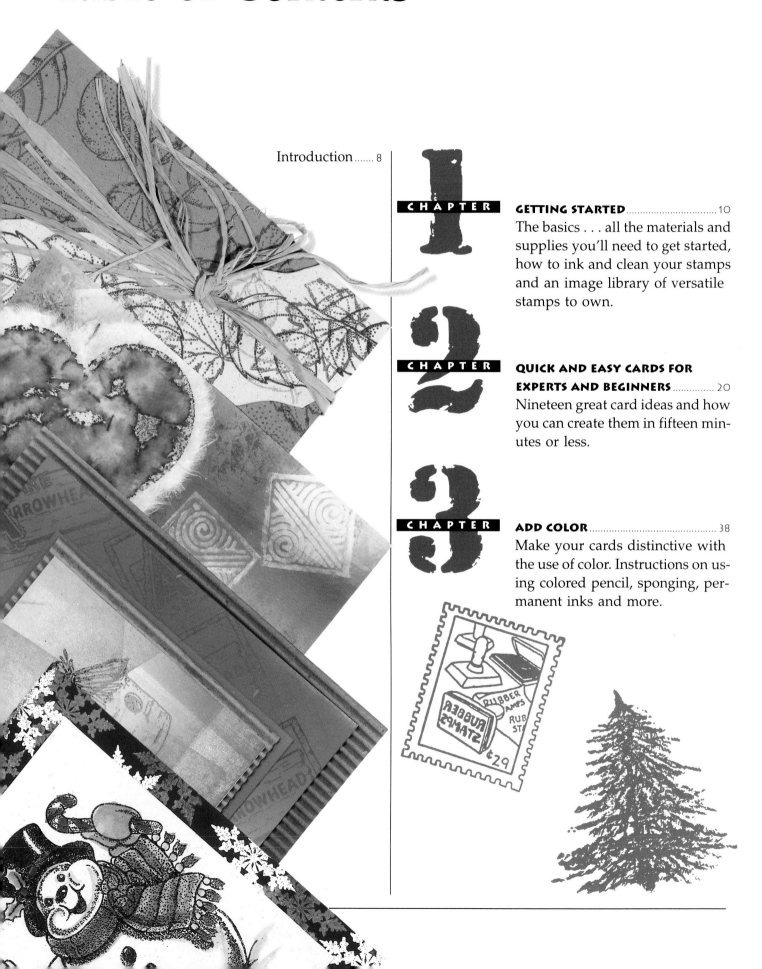

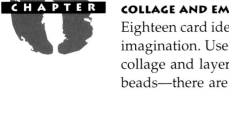

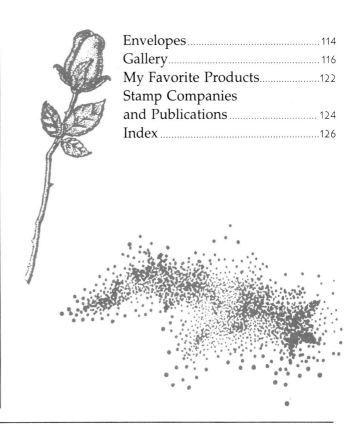

INTRODUCTION

hy rubber stamps?

Why use rubber stamps when there are so many ways to create handmade greeting cards? Satisfaction—that's the best reason I can give you. Stamps provide immediate gratification. Once you put a stamp to a pad and then to paper you're hooked. The amazing array of images available will astound you. You can make whatever you want. What other craft can say that?

Once I started stamping, I couldn't stop. First, I made quick little cards for my friends' birthdays. Before long I was on to larger pieces of work. It was so easy!

I've always been creative, but I never imagined I could work with such speed and intensity as when using rubber stamps. I've done many types of crafts but never became so involved. I think this passion is sparked by the creativity combined with the satisfaction of completing a work easily. The only struggle is deciding which images or colors to use. It is certainly easier than painting for weeks on end or throwing out projects because of mistakes or frustration. Whenever you want, you can create landscapes, portraits, surrealistic imaginings, and much more.

If you're new to stamping, please remember while doing the projects in this book that we all start from the same place; it's where you want to go that makes it worthwhile for you. For those of you already enjoying this wonderful craft, I hope there are techniques and ideas in this book that can expand your horizons. So let's begin.

CHAPTER 1

Getting Started

The basic supplies you'll need to begin making greeting cards with rubber stamps are:

Rubber stamps of course! You'll find a listing of rubber stamp companies and stores in the back of this book. Any of these stores can help you locate specific images you're looking for. Stamp pads are widely available at stamp stores, through rubber stamp companies, and at your local office supply store. Colored pencils and/or water-based markers can be found in craft and rubber-stamp stores, catalogs, variety stores, or art supply warehouses.

That's all you'll really need to get started. Many of the cards in this book can be made with just these supplies plus a few things from home, such as scissors, a craft knife, a ruler and assorted papers.

Materials

RUBBER STAMPS

I advise buying good quality stamps. There are generally three parts to a stamp—the mount, the cushion and the die. A quality mount is made from hardwood. The cushion is some type of foam that is from ⅛" to ¼" thick. The color is really of no importance. The die is the most important part of the stamp because it transfers the design. It should be closely trimmed.

A well-made stamp is a beautiful work of art. Most stamps are still made completely by hand. Please remember to buy as many stamps as you can from your local stamp shop: They need your patronage in order to stay in business. They are also the best place to learn techniques and up-to-the-minute tricks.

Most people consider stamping to be a sort of addiction, believe it! You'll buy stamps you don't really need just because you like the image. This is fun—but not very productive. You'll end up with twenty teddy bear stamps but not enough variety to make a nice complete card. So try to look for images that can develop backgrounds, words or phrases, landscape pieces like trees, mountains or fences. Think about stamps that can do more than one job. For example, a background stamp that can make a sky, or little stamps that can make borders. These stamps will serve you better in the long run than any single image stamp. You'll need a few interesting people, some animals and cute stuff like dolls or teddy bears. Flowers are always a good choice for the beginner because of their versatility. I've included an image library in this chapter to show you images that you'll find especially beneficial.

INKS

There are three basic ink types: dye, pigments and solvent. Dye-based pads are the type you see laying around the house or office. They are good to use for most papers. Pigment inks are now widely available through stamp and gift stores and are a good choice when using uncoated papers. Solvent-based inks are used mainly for stamping on unusual surfaces like wood, plastics and ceramics. I use them for a nice, crisp, black outline that won't smear like dye inks do. Solvent inks aren't for everyone. They have a tendency to smell and you must work *very* quickly.

For most beginning stampers, I recommend either dye pads and colored pencils or, for embossing, pigment pads and pens. Both techniques are simple to master and give great results.

PAPERS

Any paper, to some degree, can be stamped, so choice of paper is determined by your personal tastes. Papers fall into three categories: coated, uncoated and textured. Using different kinds of paper will add a wonderful dimension to your work, so don't be afraid to experiment.

Uncoated papers work well with all inks and I highly recommend them for beginners. These papers are readily available and come in almost every color. The vivid colors of pens are sometimes smothered if you use deep shades of uncoated paper, so if you're looking for brilliant color, stick to white or light colors, or use your pencils instead of pens since the color from pencils stays on the surface of the paper.

Textured papers include watercolor stock, handmade papers and molded papers. These types are the kind you'll love to touch, but remember their raised finishes usually make them difficult to stamp on and are generally better for backgrounds and layers.

Coated papers usually look shiny. There are a few exceptions, however. For example, JudiKins has a coated paper that has a matte-looking finish. If you're not sure if a paper is coated, use a craft knife to scrape the surface a little. The paper will be noticeably different underneath if it's coated. Coated papers are great for the bright colors of pens but aren't good for colored pencils. The coating is a poor surface for the pencil lead. Coated paper is also good for embossing with pigment inks.

NOTE CARDS

PERSONAL TRIMMER

SEE-THROUGH RULER

WATERCOLOR PAINTBRUSH

CORNER ROUNDER

CRAFT KNIFE

WATERCOLOR PENCILS

CUTTING MAT

RETRACTABLE BLADE KNIVES

MARKERS WATER-BASED

EMBOSSING POWDERS

STAMPS

CUBE STAMP

HAND CLEANER BAR

HEAT GUN

PIGMENT PAD

ZIG 2 Way Glue A

2-WAY GLUE

DYE-BASED PAD

BRAYER

Rubber Stamp Embossing Ink A001 2 fluid oz.

Extra Fine Mist Spritzer For watercolor or special effects with rubber stamps A008

Rubber Stamp Cleaner & Conditioner AC001 2 fluid oz.

Marvylous Hand Cleaning Lotion

EMBOSSING INK

SPRITZER BOTTLE

STAMP CLEANER

HAND CLEANING LOTION

Image Library

Here is a library of some good, basic images you might find useful. You'll be able to find most of these at your local stamp store; if not, the store can help you locate the designs or similar images.

Trust your own instincts and taste, but try to think ahead a little bit before you buy. Always ask yourself if this is a stamp you can use in more than one way. For example, can a part of the stamp be used as a background? By asking this kind of question, you might stop yourself from buying a stamp that you won't use.

WORDS

You won't believe how many greetings, phrases and word stamps are available. Keep your choices simple at first. Buy just the basics. Birthday greetings and general salutations are perfect beginnings.

PEOPLE

This is probably the most diverse category of images you'll come across. There are stamps of people doing just about everything. Pick the images that make you smile or laugh—an idea will be certain to follow.

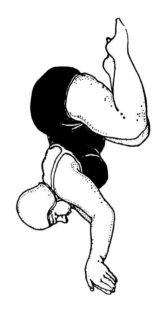

MERRY CHRISTMAS!

Congratulations!

"Celebrate"
"the"
"Season"

DESIGNS AND BACKGROUNDS

These stamps are never the first ones you buy, but they are always the ones you need after you've stamped the greeting. So, pick the designs you are drawn to—that way you'll use them. My favorites are stars. I have at least twenty different stars. I use them all the time because they're so versatile.

Image Library

LANDSCAPES

Here are a few designs you can make outdoor scenes with. This stamp is the best of many I've tried. Look twice at those mountains—they're really hippos in water. They still make great mountains.

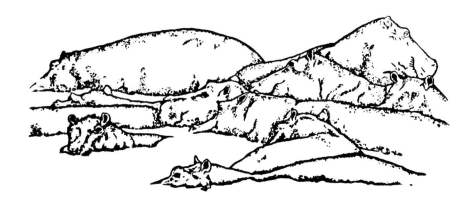

OBJECTS

In this category, look for objects that are near and dear to you and designs that you can put other things into. Luggage stamps, fishbowls or crystal balls are good examples.

IMAGES USED

Rubberstamp postoid; Rubber Baby Buggy Bumper

Celebrate the Season; Stampacadabra

Handmade Card, Congratulations; JudiKins

Merry Christmas; Carmen's Veranda

Central American cube; JudiKins

Heart burst, scrunch, solid heart; JudiKins

Question marks; Coffee Break Designs

Solid star, paper threads; JudiKins

Diving woman; Rubber Baby Buggy Bumpers

Queen; Viva Las Vegastamps

Mother; Carmen's Veranda

Grass; Hot Potatoes

Tree; Stampacadabra

Rose; Carmen's Veranda

Hippo mountains; Rubber Baby Buggy Bumpers

Pine tree; JudiKins

Hat box; Carmen's Veranda

Basic Inking and Cleaning

INK YOUR STAMP WITH A DYE-BASED PAD

Now that we've covered the essential materials we can move on to the very basic techniques of inking and cleaning your stamp:

1 Tap the stamp several times on the dye-based pad.

2 Check the rubber side to see that the raised portion is completely covered with the ink. If it is, stamp it on some scratch paper. How does it look? Did you pick up edges from the untrimmed parts of the stamp? If you did, you probably applied too much pressure. Try again. Stamp it again and again so you'll get a good feel for it. Now reink the stamp and try it on some card stock.

INK YOUR STAMP WITH A WATER-BASED MARKER

If you're just starting out, you might like to try using your water-based markers directly on the rubber die. Just color specific areas with different color markers and stamp it. Then warm it by breathing on it and stamp it again. You can usually get several impressions with one inking.

Clean Your Stamp

Before you use a different color you'll need to clean the stamp. You can clean your stamps with just water or a soap solution of half cleaner and half water. Most stamp companies have cleaners available with a scrub top. This makes it very handy. Cleaning solutions won't damage your stamps. The most damaging thing to your stamps is sunlight. I have had some stamps for fifteen years and haven't lost a single one to cleaning solutions, bleach, paint or solvent inks, so don't be afraid to try new things on your stamps.

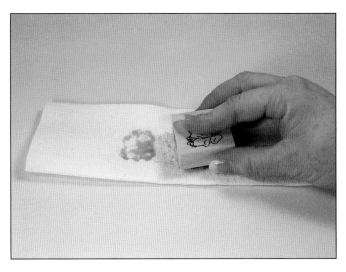

CHAPTER

Quick and Easy Cards

S ometimes the most interesting cards can be the easiest to create. You can create cards that your friends will love and your family will treasure by using simple techniques. In this chapter, I'll share some of the tricks I use to make cards quickly. These cards can be completed by even the novice stamper in about fifteen minutes.

A Simple Birthday Card

What you'll need:

1 piece white card stock, 8½″ × 5½″

1 aqua water-based pen, 1 peach pen and 1 hot pink pen

1 large frame stamp

1 Happy Birthday stamp

Lay the card stock flat with the side you are stamping facing you. Hold the large frame stamp in one hand and ink the stamp with an aqua pen. Be sure to ink it well and only put ink on the surfaces that will print. Now test the stamp on a piece of newsprint or scratch paper. Test it until you feel comfortable and get a perfect image. Reink the stamp and apply it to your card stock.

With the same aqua pen, ink the Happy Birthday stamp and repeat the same technique. Stamp on your scratch paper first and then your card. It's much easier to stamp words on the diagonal.

Begin coloring the frame. If you choose different colors from the ones here be sure they are lighter than your aqua base color. Otherwise your work may look a little muddy.

A Quick Thanks

1 Using a flower stamp or cube, stamp the flowers in red. Stamp the "Thanks" in the center.

2 Add dot accents with a black fine tip marker in between the flowers. Try not to make the dots all the same shape or size. By varying the sizes of the dots, any discrepancy in size appears normal.

Another Thank-You

1 Open a white notecard and lay it flat on your stamping surface. Using a sheet of scrap paper, mask off the bulk of the inside of the card leaving ½" border on the right-hand side.

2 Ink up the stamp in red first and stamp it along that ½" strip. Be sure to stamp the design off the edge of the paper, not only along the strip.

3 Next, with your mask still in place, wipe off the stamp and reink with black. Stamp it a few times over the area you just stamped in red. Set the card aside to dry.

4 On another piece of the same type paper, stamp the bow in red. Stamp it again on top of the image you just stamped in black.

5 Cut out the image with scissors or a craft knife. Be sure to keep the edge around the bow even. With the card closed, attach the bow with glue to the top right-hand corner. Use a Thank You stamp in the center on the face of the card. If it's difficult for you to keep word stamps straight, just stamp them on the diagonal.

Simple Border Cutouts

Here is a simple, but effective, use of a border cutout.

Cutting the same style of border on the diagonal can have a very interesting effect. Be sure that you don't cut too much off because you might want to write something on the inside.

1 This is a very easy style to make quickly. Stamp your design along the front edge of the card. Start in the middle, then continue stamping it on both sides of the first stamped design.

2 Next, use your craft knife to remove the bottom edge under the images. To add interest, you can put a contrasting color paper under that edge by using double-sided tape on the inside of the card and applying the contrasting paper to it. Add your sentiment and you're done!

Use a Cube of Stamps

These cards below are made with a cube of stamps. Four images on one stamp—what a deal! Start with a cube and some pale celadon green pigment ink. Beginning in the center of the card, stamp one of the cube images in a diagonal line across the card. Then take a gold pigment ink and, using a different side of the cube, stamp another diagonal above or below your original line.

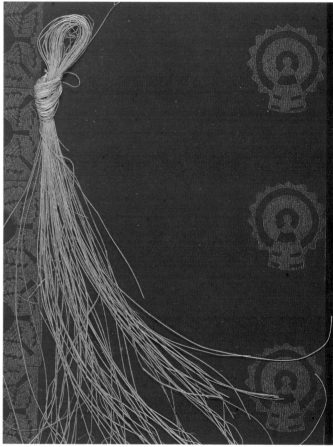

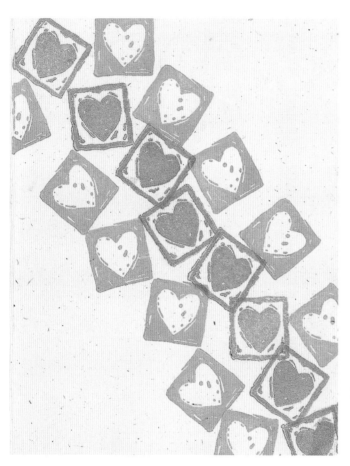

These cards also focus on using cubes. The top card on this page is stamped in two colors of pigment ink using a single side of a cube. The Celtic cross was added with a bit of raffia. The card on the opposite page is a dual border on each side of a notecard in a light pigment ink. By trimming ¼" off the face of the card and adding a deeper color on the inside with a marker, you can achieve the look of a third border. Add a little straw-like material for trimming, if you like. The bottom card is stamped with a leaf cube on the diagonal and colored in with colored pencil. Add the Happy Thanksgiving and layer-in fall colors.

Use Layering for Speedy Gift Cards

These cards are so fast to make you can do several in a day and store them for use when you need a speedy gift card.

Begin with a notecard of uncoated paper, preferably colored stock, but white will work also. Choose a stamp from your collection and stamp it all over the card. You can stamp the inside too! Take the same stamp and impress it onto the same color paper as the card. Cut that out in either a square or rectangular shape, whatever suits the shape of the stamp best. Layer this cutout onto a contrasting color of paper. It is even easier if you match the ink used to the contrast layer. Attach the two pieces together with glue or double-sided tape and apply this to the card with foam tape. Foam tape is double-sided and about ⅛" thick; it gives your cards a more dimensional look.

Try the same technique with a border. Instead of using just one impression of an image, stamp the images along a border strip of paper. Then secure the strip with glue or double-sided tape.

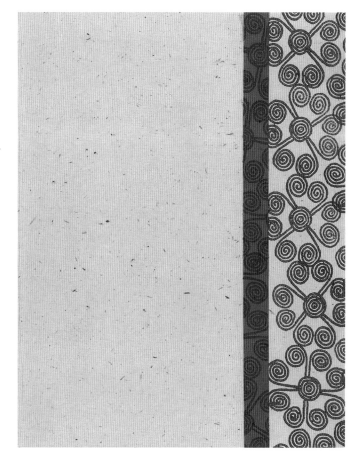

Here's an easy one: Stamp a dark colored card with faux cancellation stamps all in black inks. Lay a strip of double-sided tape down one side of the card. Lay cancelled postage from around the world on the tape and trim excess.

Build Borders

1 Stamp the card all over for a background.

2 Stamp the contrasting strip with the same pigment ink and another for contrast.

3 Layer the border with another complementary color

4 Trim it all and put it together.

Stamp It Over and Over!

Repetition and overlapping can liven up a card with color and graphic style! Use a piece of card stock approximately 4″ × 5½″. Using a rainbow pad, stamp the card over and over. Set it aside to dry. Later, stamp salutations across the front of the card in an ink darker than those you've used already. Place the piece onto white corrugated card stock. Be sure the space framing your card stock is reasonably even. Trim it carefully. The corrugated paper should stick out about ¼″ all the way around.

These three cards use ink pads and similar techniques (such as repetition and overlapping) to achieve different looks. Be sure when doing any background to go off the edges of the card.

Layer Inks

Something I found interesting about pigment inks is that they hold up even if layered on top of each other. If you stamp a metallic pigment ink and then apply a matte pigment over it, the image will almost appear three-dimensional. This also works to some extent with dye inks although the result is not nearly as crisp. The dye ink also has the tendency to bleed. This technique is especially unique when two different stamps of the same shape or style are used. Again, I've used a cube stamp for this particular card.

1 Stamp the image you've chosen in a copper pigment ink.

2 Stamp a different image over the first design in a matte brown pigment ink. Let the card dry completely. Layer the first piece onto a corrugated card.

CHAPTER 3

Happy
Mother's
Day

Hey...

Get well
soon!

Add Color

The coloring book is almost everyone's first glimpse into art. Stamping can transport you back to that blissful childhood experience.

Varieties of markers include: Fat or broad-brush to color the rubber or fill in large areas, fine- or dual-tip, foam-tip and alcohol-based. Test a few before you buy heavily into one.

You need a soft pencil without a waxy appearance for this work. I enjoy a water-soluble pencil. You can add moisture to the paper after coloring and it takes on a watercolor effect. You'll need tools that don't fall apart—there's nothing worse than a blob from a marker ruining a card. My favorite pens and pencils are listed in the back of this book. I urge you to buy the best you can afford.

Use Colored Pencils

Both of these cards were done using water-soluble pencils. You could also use regular pencils. The choice is yours.

1 Stamp your image with permanent ink or use pigment inks that have dried overnight. Now you have a good base to begin. Don't use dye-based inks or markers with water because the minute you add the water they'll run. If you have not used permanent ink before—practice, practice, practice! It's tricky because it dries so fast. You have to work faster than with any other ink.

2 Begin coloring the lightest parts first. Since many stamps have the areas to shade practically built-in, use a deeper tone of the same color in those areas that have stippling or dots, shading lines or cross-hatching.

3 Build up the color while retaining the light in your highlight areas. The highlight areas are usually the parts that have little or no shading. Put the darkest shades at the very edges of the image.

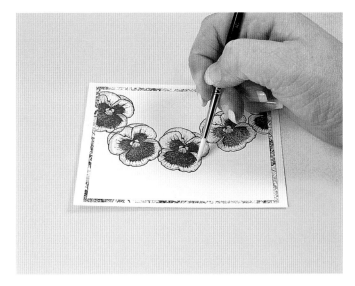

4 Dampen a watercolor brush with a little water. It shouldn't be dripping wet. Carefully apply it to the edges and blend inward. It takes practice to get really good results, so play a little before you try a gift card. For a more intense color, instead of water try deep shades of markers and blend in carefully. This is a favorite trick of mine because the result is so rich-looking.

Colored Pencil Progression

1 Stamp the image.

2 Color it with colored pencils.

3 Attach it to contrasting paper and then to corrugated paper.

Tiled Background

This technique is difficult to do with some stamps but cubes and other square stamps are simple to use because you can see the edge of the rubber. For this card I've used pigment ink. Start in the center and work out to the edges. The stamp used for the layered snowman is stamped and then colored in with pencils. Be sure to let the image dry well before applying the pencil. The whole card is put together with contrasting paper as an accent.

Here is a variation of the same snowman stamp used as a gift tag this time.

Use the Same Stamp With Different Colors

You'll use the same stamp over and over again—many times with the same color combinations. That's fine, but here's a good trick to break the habit and use your stamps for the optimum effect.

Choose two completely different color combinations. Notice the difference in the way color influences feeling. The pink card has a springtime feel and the other an autumnal look. The same stamp with a different background even works as a Christmas card. This is a simple concept but it can help when you only have a few stamps to choose from. With just the application of certain colors any stamp can be seasonal.

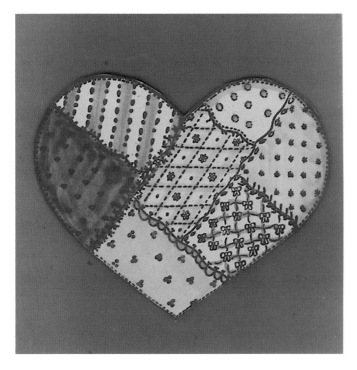

Apply Color With a Sponge

Color can be applied to large areas with many different tools—an airbrush, paintbrush, sponges or just a soft cloth. One of my favorites is the small cosmetic sponge. It's a perfect tool for adding deep color to your cards. Take the sponge in one hand and apply some color with a water-based marker to just the center of one side of the sponge. Test it on some scrap paper. If you squeeze the part of the sponge you are holding and lightly press the sponge to your paper you should come out with something similar to an airbrushed look. Practice and start with a light application of color. You can build it up as needed.

These cards show the steps progressing to the point where you stamp the greeting.

Using Permanent Inks

Many people are concerned that permanent ink will hurt the stamp. I use it all the time and I haven't lost a stamp yet to any medium, including paints and solvents. Rubber is *very* sturdy and can take any abuse except exposure to sunlight.

Many stampers don't like to use permanent ink because it can be messy and you have to work quickly. The advantages can outweigh these problems, however. One advantage is that you'll never worry about smearing again—even with watercolor! It's not for every stamper, but the depth the black permanent ink gives is well worth the trouble. You can stamp on plastic surfaces, wood and even fabric. Acetate stamping is an especially effective use for permanent ink.

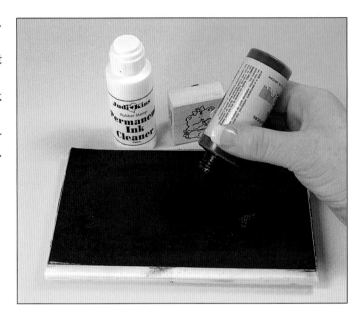

TIPS FOR USING PERMANENT INK

1 Ink your pad well. To be effective, most permanent pads will need to be reinked almost every time you use them.

2 Stamp the images on the pad and quickly check to be sure all the rubber is covered.

3 If it is well covered, stamp it a couple more times, then press it to your paper. Wait one minute. Then, color it in with anything you like. Practice and use stamps you know well at first.

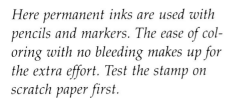

Here permanent inks are used with pencils and markers. The ease of coloring with no bleeding makes up for the extra effort. Test the stamp on scratch paper first.

Stamp With Permanent Ink on Acetate

There are some stamps that really work well on acetate. Jars and bottles, for example are obvious ones. This shopping cart was another. I wanted to be able to see what was in the cart, so acetate was the perfect choice. Stamp the image on the clear acetate and then cut it out. Layer the eggs underneath and apply the cart on top with glue.

1 Use permanent ink to stamp the shopping cart. The key to using permanent ink is to work fast.

2 Use a craft knife to cut out the parts and assemble.

Combine Techniques

Here you have the opportunity to combine a few techniques—repetitive stamping, using permanent inks and sponging. Many stampers think they can't incorporate several techniques on a single card. But you can put almost any of the ideas in this book together to make cards, so don't let someone else's rules stop you from being creative. Start this card by stamping a word diagonally across a light colored notecard. Use a couple shades of the same color pen or pad.

On white coated paper, stamp the giant TV dinner in permanent ink. Let the image dry, then color it in with markers. Always blot your work with newsprint or paper towels after coloring. That way, you reduce the chance of smearing when you touch the card. Now closely trim around the dinner and set aside. Stamp the lasso label. Sponge in color on the lasso and either stamp or write in your sentiment. Then cut it out. Remember you can use the same card design for other occasions. Apply the two cutouts to the face of the card with tape or glue. The same card could be used for Father's Day or for a new college student, just by changing the sentiment on the front.

1 *Repetitive stamping.* Stamp the word image repeat-
edly to the card. Let it overlap and go off the
edges.

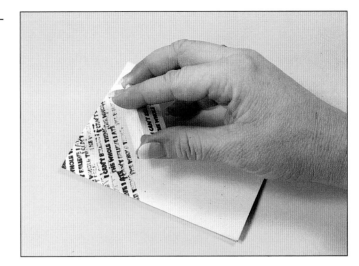

2 *Permanent ink.* Ink the stamp with permanent
ink. If it's been a while since you last used your
permanent ink you might need to refill it because it
dries so quickly. Check it before you stamp on good
paper.

3 *Sponging.* Sponge color on the lasso before
you stamp or write in your sentiment.

ARIGATO

Fabulous Cutouts

Nothing is more impressive than beautiful cut work on a greeting card. Card companies do it by machine, but you can achieve a similar look with just a craft knife and a little practice. Believe me, the response you get will be worth the extra effort!

There are several varieties and sizes of knives available—I use size no. 11 because it's versatile. You'll need enough replacement blades to change them after about ten cards. Another important tool is a metal-edged ruler. I use a see-through type to cut out frames, etc., without marking the paper. Be sure to buy one with your knife.

Hold your knife like a pencil. Put the point of the blade to the paper you are cutting and pull the blade down toward the paper. Now pull it toward you. That's all there is to it. Let's get to work!

A Simple Cut-Out Frame

Let's begin with a simple cut-out frame. Use a post-card size piece of card stock 5½″ × 4¼″. Start with the long side of the postcard and place the metal edge of the ruler on the inside of the card. There is a ½″ marking vertically and a ½″ marking horizontally on the ruler. When you line up the card vertically it should match on the horizontal lines as well. The outside edge of the card should be on the vertical ½″ mark. The first cut will begin ½″ from the top and end ½″ from the bottom of the card. Turn the card around to the opposite side and repeat the process. Now you should have two columns cut that are attached at the top and the bottom. To finish, put the ½″ vertical line on the short edge of the card with the metal edge of the ruler on the inside again, and begin your cut ½″ down and end ½″ up from the bottom. It's easy to see because your vertical cut lines on the long sides are there to guide you. Repeat the technique on the opposite side and pop out the center piece of the postcard. Try this several times on scrap paper first and you'll be an expert in no time.

Japanese Swirls. *Cutting away specific sections of a design can be very interesting if done cleanly. Simply stamp your images in a dark color of ink on dark paper. Cut away parts of the interior of the design and remount the paper onto a lighter colored notecard.*

Any card can take on an entirely different look when you use cutouts. Try cutouts to enhance a card you've already created. Sometimes it's just the thing to spice it up.

A Fancy Frame

1 Stamp the design on the front of a notecard. Be sure to get the images as near to the center as possible.

2 Using your ruler and craft knife, cut a ½″ frame. When you get to a section where you would cut through the image, stop. Begin cutting again where the frame should be.

3 The design is still attached to the card in at least two places (sometimes three or four on certain images). Cut around the stamped design in the areas not connected to the frame.

4 Back your finished card with an interesting paper or corrugated board. Use glue or double-sided tape on the backside of the frame to attach it to the card.

Here are some variations on the same theme. Frames can add life to the simplest stamped card. Try stamping any image in the center of a card and, using the same method, trim out a frame. Now that you know the basics, try a different size frame as shown on the top card. Or maybe you just need a frame to layer with a cut-out image as shown on the bottom card.

More Seasonal Cutouts

One of the best ways to use cutouts in rubber stamping is to completely cut around an image and use glue or mounting tape to attach it to a previously stamped background. Look at this easy Easter card. This card is quick to finish and it's easy to duplicate for any season simply by changing the background. This method is effective on designs that you want to pop out—for example, the stick arms on the quilted snowman. If you carefully add a double thickness of mounting tape at the ends of the arms, they will appear to be reaching for you.

Here's an easy Hanukkah card. Simply cut out the gelt and apply a double thickness of mounting tape. Stamp your greeting in the background and you're done.

Choose solid pumpkin designs. You can always cut out jack-o-lantern faces and with the solid pumpkins you will still be able to use the stamps for Thanksgiving and fall cards.

Sunflower Cut-Out Card

What you'll need:

    1 piece of yellow card stock, 4" × 6"

    1 piece of corrugated card stock, 8½" × 5½"

    1 large flower stamp

    1 brown stamp pad (pigment or dye ink) or pen

    colored pencils

    scissors

    foam mounting tape

To give this card a little added interest, stamp an extra flower image onto a lighter yellow card stock and cut out just the flower heads. Color the heads as you did before, then use mounting tape to affix these onto the image you've already colored on the darker yellow card stock. Attach all of this to the corrugated card.

1 Ink the flower stamp and test it on scratch paper. Once you've checked it, stamp it on the yellow card stock. Let it dry thoroughly, especially if you've used pigment ink. While you wait, fold the corrugated stock in half.

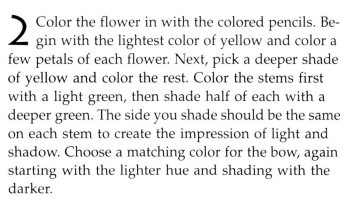

2 Color the flower in with the colored pencils. Be-gin with the lightest color of yellow and color a few petals of each flower. Next, pick a deeper shade of yellow and color the rest. Color the stems first with a light green, then shade half of each with a deeper green. The side you shade should be the same on each stem to create the impression of light and shadow. Choose a matching color for the bow, again starting with the lighter hue and shading with the darker.

3 With your scissors, trim the yellow card stock around the stamped edge. I usually leave about ⅛" all the way around whatever I'm cutting. Apply the mounting tape to the back of your yellow card stock. Remove the release film from the tape and firmly secure the yellow card stock to the corrugated card.

Colossal Cutouts

If you like to buy the big stamps, this is a project for you! I especially like the fruit and vegetable ones. Begin with images that are at least 3"×3". Smaller "big stamps," also shown here, are best suited to gift tags. These cards are easy because they only take one stamp.

Ink up a big stamp. Then stamp as close to the folded edge of a notecard as you can.

Using a craft knife, cut through both layers of the card as close to the design as possible without cutting through the image on the side with the fold. Be sure to leave at least a generous inch on the fold—the card will be more stable that way.

These cards make great invitations, gift tags or baby announcements, just to name a few of the possibilities. They also are very quick to make. Stamp them all one night and cut them out the next day.

1 Stamp the design on a notecard. Make sure you stamp the image right on the folded edge.

2 Cut out the design, leaving the folded edge intact. If you want the card to stand, use a ruler to trim the bottom straight. Trim just enough to make it stand, trying not to cut off too much of the image.

CHAPTER 5

The Magic of Masking

Masking is one of the most intriguing techniques in rubber stamping. It is both simple and dramatic. In fact, it's so simple that masking is often overlooked in favor of more technically challenging methods of stamping. Just as the word implies, it involves covering up an image with paper so that other designs can be stamped over it, giving the illusion of perspective. Master this technique if you're new to stamping. Everyone finds a beautifully masked greeting fascinating.

Masking Tips

The paper you use to make a mask is important. It needs to be lightweight and uncoated. For example, tracing paper, newsprint, typing paper or Post-its work well. I generally use newsprint because it's so absorbent, can be cut to any size and is inexpensive. Many mask makers use Post-its but I don't care for them because of the size limitations. They are convenient but you can use any two-way glue and derive the same convenience. If you let the two-way glue dry before you place the mask it becomes a temporary bond that can be re-positioned. You can also use removable tape to hold the mask in place.

When you decide on colors for the images, choose the darkest inks for the foreground and lighter inks for the backgrounds. The background images will blend away with the dark ink of the original image in case your mask doesn't quite do the job. Also, don't color in the image until you've stamped the basic background. That way you can fill in with a deeper color if the mask didn't cover the image or you cut too much off the mask.

There are times that you won't need to cut a complete mask. For example, if the background is only on one side of the image just cut half a mask. There are other times when just a piece of torn paper will do for a mask. This works well on images that are graphic in nature. Torn paper can also make an interesting sky or grassy knoll, just by sponging a little color over it onto your card.

For making a more lasting mask, permanent ink on acetate is great. Stamp an image in permanent ink onto acetate and let it dry well. Cut it out carefully, just inside the lines. Now you have a mask to use over and over that you can see through. I do this for certain stamps that I use often, especially if I'm making more than ten of a particular card. It's perfect for ink that isn't permanent, because the ink just wipes right off.

Like many stamping techniques, masking takes some practice but the results are well worth the extra effort.

1 Begin by choosing a stamp with simple lines or a basic geometric shape. Stamp the image on a notecard and set the card aside. Stamp the same image on the masking paper.

2 Cut out the image just inside the original line of the design. This eliminates the shadow an oversized mask can leave around the original stamped image. Lay the mask directly on the image. At this point you should be able to see a slight outline of the image from under the mask.

3 Now choose your background stamp and stamp it all around the mask.

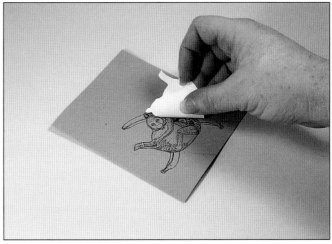

4 Pull up the mask. That's it!

Make a Doggie in the Window Card

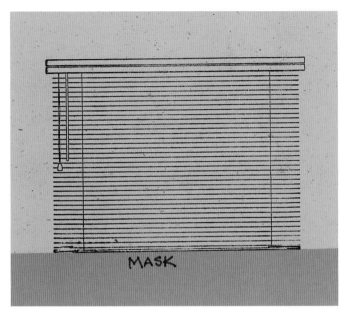

1 Stamp the mini blind design in the center of a card and set aside. Place a piece of masking paper just below the image.

2 Ink up the dog stamp and stamp it on the bottom edge, half of it on the mask and half on the mini blind image.

3 Pull up the mask. Put in color and decoration.

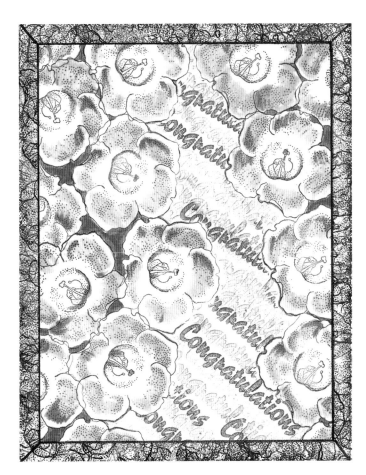

Here are three more examples of simple masking. When masking a stamped image, you need to visualize the foreground first. That means the first image you stamp is in the front and everything else follows after that image is masked.

Use a Mask and Reverse Mask

Here is an example of an intricately masked card using a mask and a reverse mask.

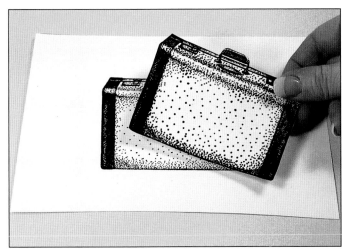 

1 Stamp the suitcase in the center of a large post-card; set this aside. Create a large mask for it and save the outside mask as well. This is known as the reverse mask. Cut carefully so you won't be doing double work. This time cut exactly on the image lines and then trim a little off of each mask.

2 Using the first mask over the suitcase, stamp luggage tags and travel decals around the suitcase. Let this dry well.

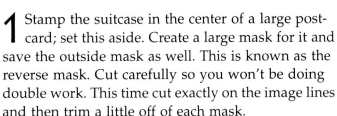

3 Lay the reverse mask over those images you just stamped. Take the decal background and ink it up, then stamp it several times over the suitcase. Be sure to use the same color or a lighter color ink to stamp the background so it will blend with the ink used for the suitcase.

4 Color with pens and sponging. Reuse the reverse mask to sponge in color just where you want it. I used permanent ink on some of the images to be able to easily color in without smearing.

Use Masks for Perfect Postage Frames

One of my favorite stamping creations is also one of the quickest to make—faux postage. It really only involves simple masking and is so easy because of the geometric shape of most postage.

There are many postage frames available, in a wide range of sizes and styles. Many stamp companies have a good variety, and stamp stores usually carry several types. Look for a postage frame with a heavier line on the inside of the frame. That way, if you stamp the frame in a dark color this thicker line will be easier to mask.

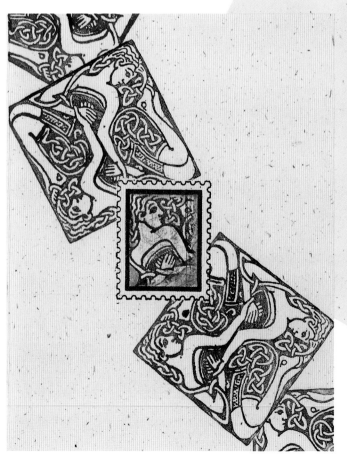

1 Begin by choosing a blank postage frame. Stamp it in black permanent ink or any other dark ink onto a white postcard. Now stamp the frame onto a piece of masking paper and cut out the center of the frame. Remember to overcut the mask slightly so there won't be that gap between the image you stamp and the frame.

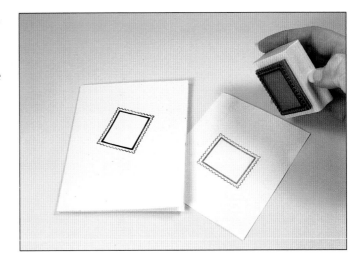

2 Choose a stamp for the center and, with the mask in place, stamp your image. I used permanent ink on some of the images to be able to easily color in without smearing.

3 Pull up the mask. Color your work with markers or pencils.

CHAPTER 6

Best
Wishes

Collage and Embellishments

Collage greeting cards are some of the most interesting and elegant cards. Using a little scrap of handmade paper here and a stamp or two there you can turn a blank card into a treasure. These are good choices for general card use—pull one out when you need it, add the sentiment, and it's perfect for any occasion. They also make a lovely gift in a matching collage box.

Here are a few tips: Limit your palette to three colors so you won't go overboard. This still allows for creativity. Keep your stamp choice to a minimum. Use the same design in two different sizes—the bigger as the focal point, the smaller as a background. Coordinated designs (like cubes) are great for this style.

Look in craft, antique and stamp stores for odd embellishments. Many stamp stores and companies sell collage kits.

Dual-Tone Look

This look is very subtle and great for the cultural images used here. It also works well for large word stamps.

1 Ink up one half of a graphic style stamp with gold pigment ink. Now ink the other half of the stamp with copper pigment ink.

2 Stamp the image onto a dark card. Don't clean the stamp until you're completely finished with this combination of colors. This technique is best when the inks have blended together a bit. If the ink pads get a little mixed, gently wipe off the tops with a paper towel.

These two cards are perfect for the dual-tone look with a little layering. Begin with dual-toned parts—the hands and backgrounds—then layer them. Stamp up several hands in different sizes and a couple of postcards with simple backgrounds. Keep the colors of paper limited to two shades. Now you have coordinated pieces to make cards with.

Ethnic Card Designs

All of these cards use a variety of the techniques discussed in previous chapters. The techniques have been adapted for an ethnic look using images of graphic designs from around the world.

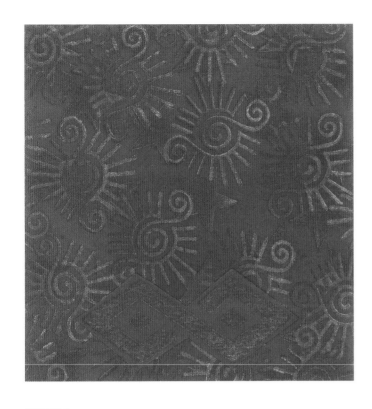

Collage and Layers

You can build collage-style cards quickly with the right ingredients. Layering is an easy technique to use. Stick to odd numbers of layers and you can never go wrong. Odd numbers are more pleasing to the eye. I try to make at least three and no more than five layers. Alternate two colors of paper usually with the darkest color on the bottom. You can reuse this recipe with almost any type of notecard or postcard. These two cards have a more puritan style using plain geometric shapes.

The most basic layering is at times the best. A simple square layered onto a notecard leaves enough room at the bottom of the card for a message or maybe a tiny border.

This trick works with most stamps: Stamp a single image on the same color paper as the card. Trim or cut a geometric shape around the image. Glue that piece on a coordinating color of paper and trim, leaving a ¼" edge.

These two cards are intriguing. Unusual elements and fibrous papers combined in an asymmetrical manner give a unique appearance, even though the same layering method is used. This type of card seems to get a lot of attention because it is askew.

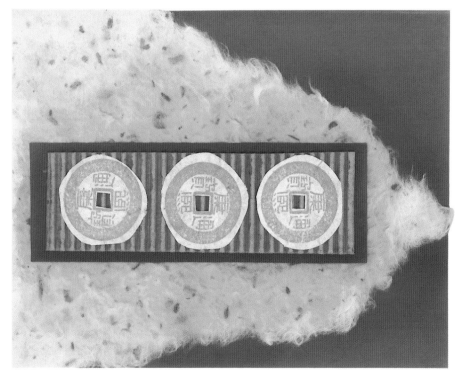

Embellishments

There are times when a card might need something extra. Dig into your box of craft stuff and look for anything that can be attached with a little glue—beads, sequins, raffia, yarn—the list is endless. On the four cards shown here I've used shells, raffia and other fibers for accent. Of course, if you're doing cute or Victorian cards you might glue on ribbons or feathers instead.

Keep in mind the type of greeting you're going for. Simple cards call for simple accents, and when it comes to embellishments less is more. Also, remember you are working on paper and the weight of some items might be too much for a lightweight notecard.

On this card the accent is simple—a single shell with fiber ribbon tied through it. A nice touch for a basic card.

Three shells and a fiber border is all it takes to finish this card. Sticking to odd numbers is an easy formula to follow for most projects, especially when it comes to embellishments.

A wide border at the edge of this card is accented with a bit of raffia. Raffia can be tied on a card or glued on.

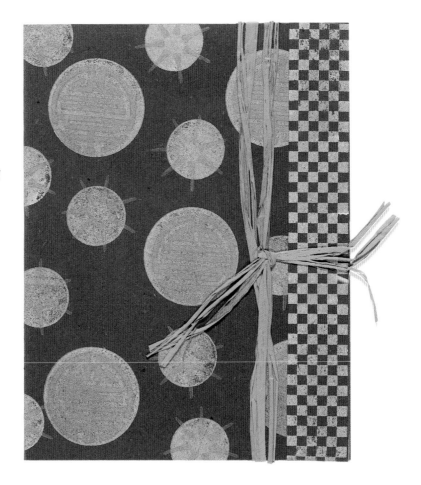

Here again a single shell and a little rope add an interesting border to a quickly stamped card.

Stamping on Rubber

Many stampers are attracted to the bold look of solid stamps. These are the stamps that can, at times, frustrate beginners. Often these stamps repel ink when you first use them because they have so much rubber on the surface. Before you start, clean the stamp with a solvent-type cleaner, then buff the surface of the rubber lightly with a pumice stone and clean again. This should remove anything left on the rubber from the vulcanizing process.

Start with a large solid stamp. A heart is perfect for this project. Ink the stamp with a couple of markers. Quickly ink a smaller stamp with pigment ink and apply it to the surface of the large stamp. Now you have applied a pattern to the solid stamp. Give the large stamp a blast of hot breath to revive the marker ink and stamp it on an uncoated postcard. If you have a fine mist spritzer bottle lightly spray a little water on the rubber and stamp again on another card.

1 Apply marker to the stamp. Try a couple of colors on the rubber.

2 Ink the second stamp with pigment ink and stamp it onto the first large stamp.

3 Spritz a little water on the rubber and you can stamp again.

CHAPTER 7

Embossing

mbossing has a professional look and makes even a simple rubber-stamp design elegant. It's easy if you have the right tools and know how to use them.

Embossing fluid is usually a clear pigment ink, but sometimes it's slightly tinted. It's perfect for certain colors of embossing powders. However, if you own pigment inks don't rush to buy embossing ink. Try your pigment inks first. Pigments work for embossing because they dry slowly. Other inks don't work consistently, so I recommend pigments only.

You can emboss on any paper but your best bet is coated stock. Buy good quality embossing powder—finely ground that doesn't cling too much to coated papers. The powder sticks to the image because the ink remains wet. Prevent excessive static cling because once the powder is heated you can't remove it.

Embossing: Step-by-Step

1 Assemble notecards, pigment ink, embossing powder, a heat source and a rubber stamp to begin. Ink your stamp. Some stamps emboss better than others. Always do a test on scratch paper first. Press the stamp to the card.

2 Pour the powder over the image. Be generous. It's better to cover the image with a whole jar than to sprinkle the powder and not get good coverage.

3 Shake off the excess powder and pour it back into the jar. Tap the card gently but firmly to take off any remaining powder that is not clinging to the wet ink.

4 Heat the powder thoroughly until it melts. If it has an orange-peel look, it's not heated enough. Heat it quickly once more. You can now color it in with pens or leave uncolored for a purely elegant look.

There are a variety of methods to heat the powder. Many people use an iron or toaster oven. These methods are fine, especially at first while deciding whether to invest in a heat gun. Start with whatever heating source you may have such as a hot plate or coffee warmer because they provide a slow cooking method. But a heat gun can't be beat when it comes to speed and ease. Be sure you like embossing before you invest in a heat gun—and *no*, a hairdryer won't work!

Embossing Examples

Three Leaves. *Use a leaf stamp or cube and stamp it in gold pigment ink. Pour light gold powder over the images, emboss as described on the previous pages. Color the leaves in fall shades of reds, rusts and oranges. Carefully cut out the leaves. Place a circle of rope fibers on the card with strong glue and attach the leaves to the card with mounting tape.*

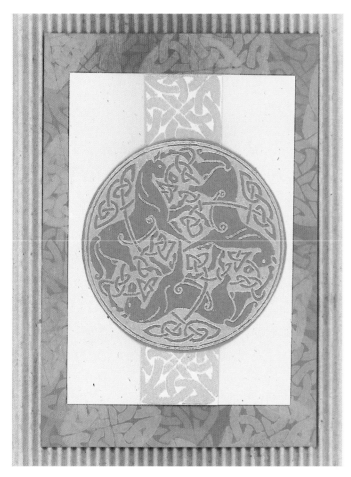

Celtic Medallion. *Stamp the image in gold or copper pigment ink and then emboss with metallic gold powder. I used a matching Celtic cube in the background. Sometimes very solid rubber stamps are difficult to emboss. The most common problem is not enough ink on the stamp. Ink the stamp up taking care to cover the entire surface of the rubber.*

Celestial Suns. *For this card I used black pigment ink with clear powder. Clear powder takes on the color of whatever ink is underneath. So it is an excellent choice when you are trying to match paper and ink.*

More Embossed Greetings

There is a wide variety of embossing powders available. These cards show a few of the basic types.

"Be My Valentine" is done with a clear-based sparkle powder with gold and pinks underneath. This is a nice look for a wedding card as well.

"Happy Easter" is black ink with a deep gray powder. This combination achieves a softer look than using black on black.

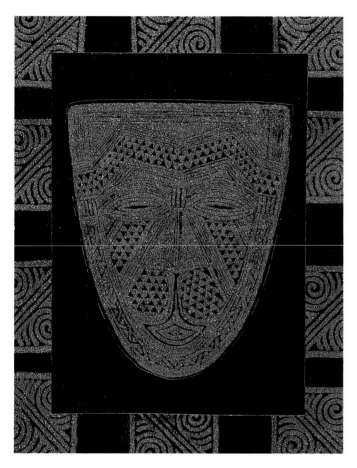

This "Egyptian Mask" card is done in a sparkle gold, called Egyptian Gold, from JudiKins. It just may be my favorite powder.

The sun in this "Sun and Stars" card is done in a black sparkle powder with black ink underneath.

Dual-Color Embossing

This is not a new technique but it is one people forget
to use. It is especially effective for images that really
call for a two-color outline.

1 You'll need pigment ink and a clear-base embossing powder for this project. First decide on the
two colors to use (I used red and black in this example). Ink up the lighter of the two colors first. Then
ink the remainder of the image in the second color.
Check the rubber to be sure all of the stamp is inked.

2 Stamp the image on the selected paper and immediately pour the embossing powder over the
entire design. Remember to be generous with the
powder to get good coverage. Now heat the powder.
Let the newly embossed image set for a moment. If
you are coloring in the image, remember to carefully
select colors that are lighter than the two colors
you've used for the outline of the design.

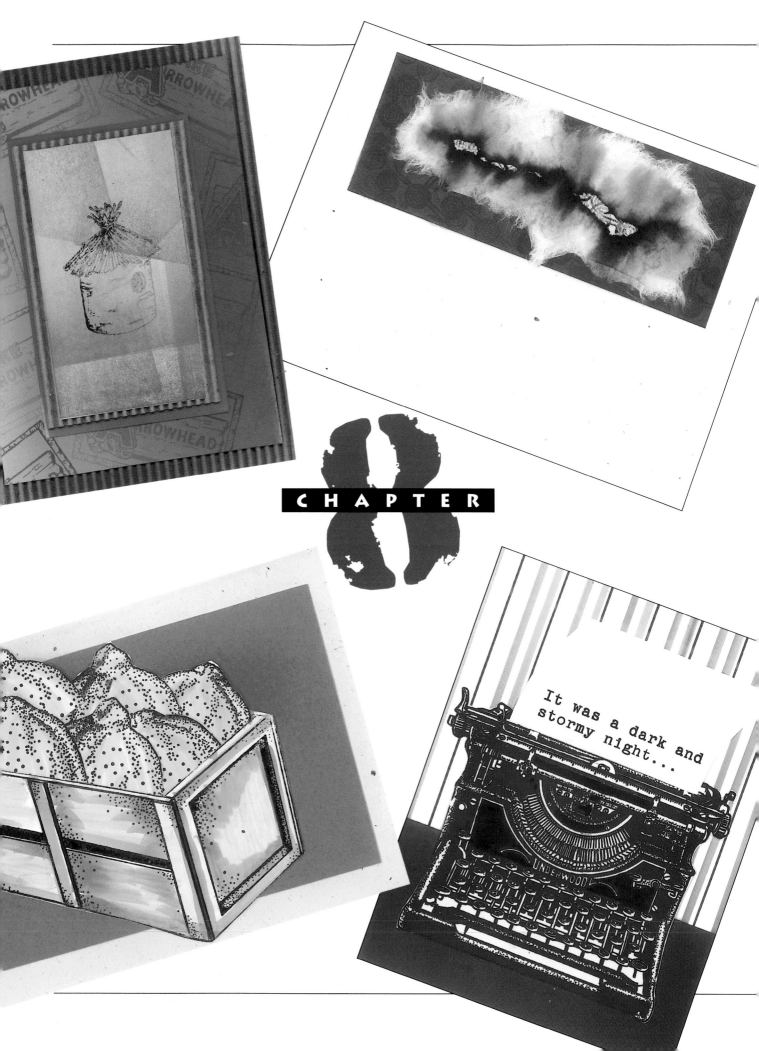

CHAPTER 8

Special Effects

The tricks and techniques in this chapter are a little more challenging than some of the previous ideas. We'll make water-stained cards, learn to use a brayer, and employ a cutting technique to create cards with slots. Because there is really no correct way to complete these types of cards, you'll need to uncover your own creativity and artistic instinct.

Begin by teaching yourself how to play again. Take out those stamps just to play with them. Play around with the ideas in this chapter to come up with a card or idea that pleases you!

Water Staining

1 Choose a graphic image and ink it with a dye-based pad or marker. Stamp it on handmade paper. Reink your stamp with a pigment ink in a deeper tone. Stamp it right over your first image. It shouldn't be perfect—if the design is off by ¼" or less, it will work really well.

2 Using a fine mister or a paint brush apply a little water. Watch as the dye-based ink bleeds on the paper. This is out of your control so just let it happen.

3 If you are happy with the result—stop. If you want to go a little farther you can stamp the pigment ink over the design again maybe with a metallic ink or stamp a smaller design over the entire piece.

1 To retain a feathery edge on handmade paper, use your paint brush and some water to outline the shape you want around the stamped design.

2 Tear the paper by gently pulling it where you have applied the water. Take your time, especially if the paper is still wet from the water-staining process. The paper should tear in the shape you marked with the water. If it doesn't, let the piece dry completely, then try again.

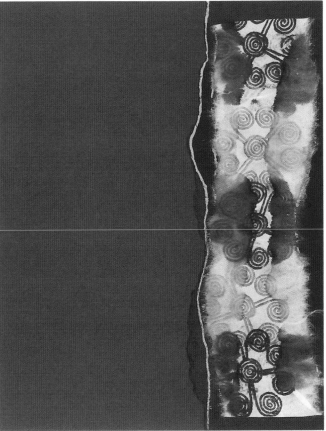

3 Let your work dry well. When it is dry, use double-sided tape or mounting tape to adhere the piece to your card. I like to make several designs in different color combinations to be used later on cards and envelopes.

More Water-Staining Ideas

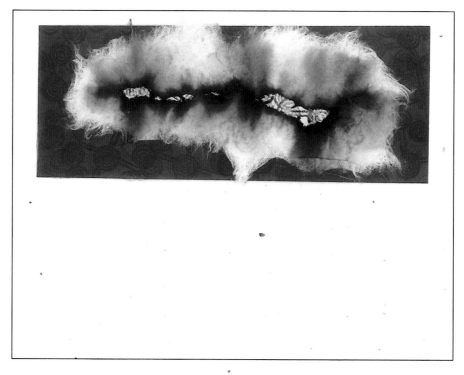

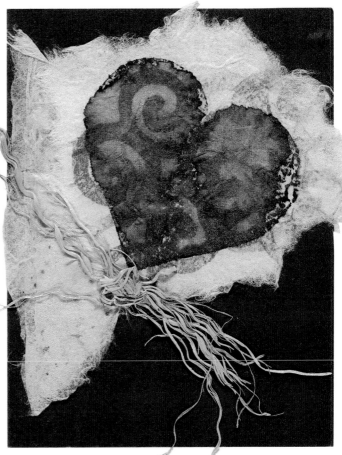

Using a Brayer . . .

A brayer is like a rubber rolling pin. There are several styles and sizes. Be sure to get a soft rubber brayer for rubber stamping rather than a hard brayer used in printmaking. Soft rubber brayers take the ink well and work on the papers that stampers use.

1 Set the ink pad horizontally in front of you. Place the brayer on the pad and roll it in one continuous motion. Do not roll it back and forth because this only inks half the brayer. When you get to the end of the pad, lift and begin again. It takes practice. Coated stock paper works best when using a brayer. It really soaks up the ink so be sure to use enough.

2 Roll the brayer back and forth across the paper. Continue rolling until there is only a little ink left. Then reink and try it again. The amount of coverage on the paper is up to you.

If there are lines on the paper, you may have hit the edge of the pad when inking the brayer. Try to avoid the edges as much as possible. Blend the edges on the card where the brayer was not used by applying the ink to the paper with a slight zigzag motion. Don't zigzag too much or you'll have a muddy mess.

With Stamps

You can achieve a batik or resist look by applying embossing fluid to your stamp and stamping on MatteKote paper, (a coated paper with a matte finish) before brayering. This technique only works well on MatteKote because the images come out clear. With other papers the look is not nearly as clean.

1 Apply embossing fluid to a stamp and stamp the image on card stock.

2 Brayer over the wet embossing fluid you've just stamped. If you don't have embossing fluid, you can use a light color of pigment ink in the same manner. You'll see the images almost immediately. The images have a ghostly quality to them so this is a perfect trick for a Halloween card, too.

Blending With the Brayer

There are times when you might want the colors to blend in a different combination while using the brayer and rainbow pad. To achieve this, just brayer half the card, turn the paper around and blend the matching colors together by brayering the other half. This will give you a bright band of color down the center of the paper.

The brayering on these cards was done using the same methods. If you don't care for rainbow pads, try using markers on the brayer. Stripes or just blotches of color are especially effective.

Cards With Slots

Here's a cute card using techniques previously described with the addition of mounting tape and some
extra cut work. The same idea can be used to create
gift boxes or open books. In fact, any stamp that has
a center to cut out can be used with the same technique. Always consider the everyday items you can
put to use in your stamping. This card would be quite
ordinary without the wax paper.

1 Stamp the lunchbox in a dark brown marker or pad. Carefully color with colored pencils and set aside. Now stamp and cut out the lunch items: an apple, a milk bottle and a sandwich.

2 With a craft knife, cut out just the center of the inside of the lunchbox.

3 Using double-sided tape, place the piece cut out of the center in position on a notecard. Apply mounting tape in several areas on the back of the lunchbox. Now position it over the center piece already in place.

4 The mounting tape should give a 3-D effect and a built in pocket for a small bit of crumpled wax paper. Stamp a sentiment to the left of the lunchbox.

More Cards With Slots

Lobster Lunch. *Here I used the same 3-D technique except I didn't completely glue the lobsters down. The card has a bit more texture to it because some of the tails have been left up. Be sure to securely attach the parts that are glued, though. You don't want them to fall off if touched.*

Great Crate. *Here is an example of another great stamp for mounting tape. This crate has a perfect section to cut out and add in a few fruits or veggies. If you like, try a double or triple layer of mounting tape for extra height. Then layer in the fruit on single pieces of tape. If you are mailing it, check with the post office—you might need extra postage for the thickness.*

Use Your Imagination

A typewriter stamp like this one gives you a card for any occasion. Here a slot was added so that a piece of paper with a message could be slipped in. This is done very simply with a craft knife and a ruler.

Stamp the typewriter in black pigment or permanent ink. Cut it out and set it on a cutting board. Place a see-through ruler with a metal edge on the area to be cut. Slice through a section of the typewriter but leave enough space on either end so that the edges can be glued down.

Insert a piece of typing paper with your message through the slot. This piece can be permanently affixed or be left loose so the recipient can remove the note to keep as a reminder. Now tape or glue the typewriter to a notecard or a background like this one. For a striped wall like the one shown here, use the ruler and a fine tip marker.

The pleasure of a dog is that you may make a fool of yourself with him and not only will he not scold you, but he will make a fool of himself too. *Samuel Butler*

As you can see, slots can be very versatile for applying many stamped pieces. Let your imagination run wild!

Envelopes

Finally, we come to the part of your card that the receiver sees first—the envelope. Create an envelope that complements your card, but keep it simple. The greeting card should not be overshadowed by the envelope.

An envelope can match your card but does not necessarily have to match it exactly. It can be a different color or use completely different stamps. Do keep something about it similar to the card, though. The ink color can tie it together perhaps, or use at least one stamp from the card.

Use your stamp on one side of the envelope and, for additional interest, continue the image along the flap.

The only thing domestic about me is that I was born in this country.

Use a variation of the main image on the card to create continuity and a little foreshadowing.

Vellum is great to use for envelopes. In this example, color in the teddy bear angel so that, when the card is inserted, the "Salutations" and snowflakes show through the vellum.

Here is another example of an effective use of vellum for an envelope. Embossing on the vellum adds a sophisticated touch.

Gallery

On the following pages is a gallery of cards made with the techniques covered in this book. Many of these cards can be copied but go ahead and try to adapt them to stamps you own or to styles you would like to try and expand your creativity. Have fun!

With love
and
warm fuzzys!

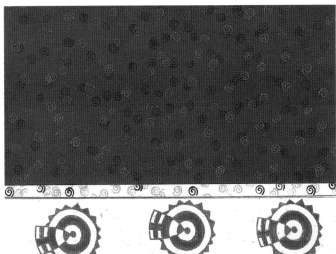

BYOB
BRING YOUR OWN BOOTS!
You're Invited!

For A WILD WEST BRUNCH
Date JULY 26TH
Time 9³⁰ AM
Place MY HOUSE
9020 WEST DR
RSVP 555 -6384
Hosted By ME

Gallery

Warmest Christmas wishes from our house to yours.

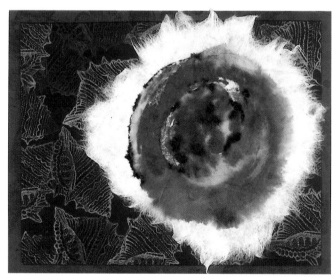

Gallery

My Favorite Products

STAMP SUPPLIES

Listed here are some stamping items that I enjoy using and which work well for me:

See-Thru ruler by JudiKins

Staedtler pens and watercolor pencils

All papers used in this book including MatteKote and Ultra papers by JudiKins

Embossing powders by JudiKins

Rainbow pads by Alice in Rubberland

Name and address stamps by Coffee Break Designs

STAMPS

Here is a listing of the stamps used in this book by page number:

22-26 all stamps by JudiKins

28 cube stamp by Alice in Rubberland

29 all stamps and fibers by JudiKins

30 top card stamps by Stampacadabra
bottom card stamps by Carmen's Veranda

31 top card stamps by JudiKins
bottom card stamps and postage stamps by Carmen's Veranda

32-35 all stamps by JudiKins

40,41 stamps by JudiKins

42,43 stamps by Rubbermoon

44-47 all stamps by JudiKins

49 top left and bottom stamps by Judikins
top right stamps by Rubber Baby Buggy Bumpers
middle card stamps by Carmen's Veranda

50 stamps by Carmen's Veranda

52,53 stamps by Carmen's Veranda

56 all stamps by JudiKins

57 top card stamps by JudiKins
bottom card tooth fairy stamp by Stampacadabra
swirl by JudiKins

60 top card stamps by JudiKins
bottom card stamps by Carmen's Veranda

61 stamps by Carmen's Veranda

62,63 stamps by Worth Repeating

62,63 teacup stamp by Hot Potatoes
surprised guy by Love You To Bits
angel by Stampacadabra
crystal ball by Carmen's Veranda
mother and daughter by Moe Wubba
ear of corn by Carmen's Veranda

70,71 stamps by JudiKins

72,73 stamps by Carmen's Veranda

74,75 stamps by JudiKins

78-87 stamps and fibers by JudiKins

90-95 stamps by JudiKins

96,97 stamps by Stampacadabra

100-107 stamps by JudiKins

108-113 stamps by Carmen's Veranda

114 left, envelope stamp by JudiKins
address stamp by Coffee Break Designs;
right, card stamps by Viva Las Vegastamps
matching envelope postage frames by Judikins

115 stamps by JudiKins

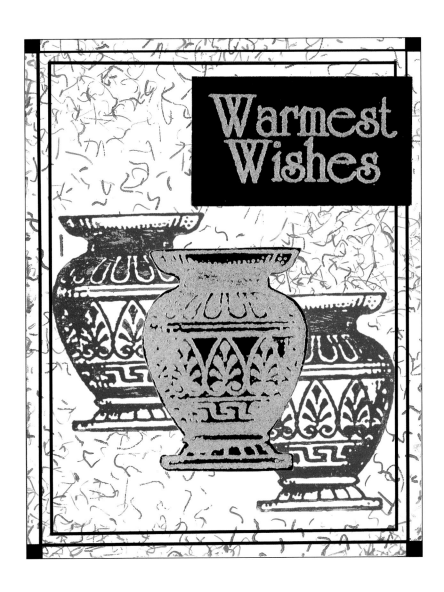

Stamp Companies and Publications

The companies in this directory sell high quality rubber stamps. All those listed have different policies regarding catalogs, stamps and supplies. You can write or call them for information.

Alice in Rubberland
P.O. Box 9262
Seattle, WA 98109

Art Gone Wild
800-945-3980

A Stamp in the Hand
20630 S. Leapwood Avenue, Suite B
Carson, CA 90746
310-329-8555

Carmen's Veranda
187-C W. Orangethorpe Avenue
Placentia, CA 92670
714-993-3264

Coffee Break Designs
P.O. Box 34281
Indianapolis, IN 46234

Hot Potatoes
209 10th Avenue, Suite 311
Nashville, TN 37203
615-255-4055

JudiKins
17832 S. Hobart Boulevard
Gardena, CA 90248
310-515-1115

Love You to Bits
P.O. Box 5748
Redwood City, CA 94063
800-546-LYTB

Moe Wubba
P.O. Box 1445
San Luis Obispo, CA 93406
805-547-1MOE

Museum of Modern Rubber
3015 Glendale Boulevard, Suite 100C
Los Angeles, CA 90039
213-662-1133

Ruby Red Rubber
P.O. Box 2076
Yorba Linda, CA 92686
714-970-7584

Rubber Baby Buggy Bumpers
1331 W. Mountain Avenue
Fort Collins, CO 80521
970-224-3499

Rubbermoon
P.O. Box 3258
Hayden Lake, ID 83835

Stampacadabra
2824 W. Ashlan Avenue, Suite 104
Fresno, CA 93705
209-227-7247

Stampscapes
7451 Warner Avenue, #E124
Huntington Beach, CA 92647

Stamps Happen, Inc.
369 S. Acacia Avenue
Fullerton, CA 92631
714-879-9894

Stamp Oasis
4750 W. Sahara Avenue, Suite 17
Las Vegas, NV 89102
800-234-TREK

Viva Las Vegastamps
330 Decatur Boulevard, Suite 226
Las Vegas, NV 89107

Wizard of Ah's Stamps
4538 W. Lord Redman Loop
Tucson, AZ 85741

Worth Repeating
227 N. East Street
New Auburn, WI 54757
715-237-2011

STAMPING PUBLICATIONS
For more information on stamping or stores in your area, try these stamping publications:

National Stampagraphic
19652 Sacramento Lane
Huntington Beach, CA 92646-3223
714-968-4446

RUBBERSTAMPMADNESS
408 S.W. Monroe, #210
Corvallis, OR 97330
541-752-0075

Stamper's Sampler
21085 Jenner
Lake Forest, CA 92630
714-380-7318

Vamp Stamp News
P.O. BOX 386
Hanover, MD 21076-0386

Index